CARS

FERRARI

Michael Bradley

Marshall Cavendish
Benchmark
New York

Marshall Cavendish Benchmark
99 White Plains Road
Tarrytown, NY 10591
www.marshallcavendish.us

Library of Congress Cataloging-in-Publication Data

Bradley, Michael, 1962-
  Ferrari / by Michael Bradley.
    p. cm. — (Cars)
  Includes index.
  ISBN 978-0-7614-2978-4
  1. Ferrari automobile—History—Juvenile literature. 2. Ferrari, Enzo,
1898—1988—Juvenile literature. 3. Automobile
engineers—Italy—Biography—Juvenile literature. I. Title.
TL215.F47B73 2009
629.222'2—dc22
2007047829

Photo research by Connie Gardner

Cover photo by Ron Kimball/www.kimballstock.com

The photographs in this book are used by permission and through the courtesy of: Ron Kimball/www.
kimballstock.com: back cover, 9, 16, 26(T & B); Corbis: Car Culture, 1, 19; Bettmann, 12; Schlegelmilch, 13, 25;
PhotoEdit: Spencer Grant, 29; Alamy: Phil Talbot, 5, 24(B), 28; Transtock, 17; imagebroker, 2; AP Photo: 7, 8,
14, 20; The Image Works: Topham, 10; Getty Images: Car Cuture, 18, 21; Mike Hewitt, 24(T); Cameron Spencer, 27.

Publisher: Michelle Bisson
Art Director: Anahid Hamparian
Series Designer: Daniel Roode

Printed in Malaysia
1 3 5 6 4 2

CONTENTS

CHAPTER ONE
HUMBLE BEGINNINGS

The office was bone cold, and the December chill **invaded** without mercy. A single bulb hung above Enzo Ferrari's desk, providing minimal light. It was Christmas Eve, 1946, and the president and founder of the race car construction company Auto Avio Construzione in Maranello, Italy, had a late visitor. Ferrari had struggled since the end of World War II. Work had been hard to find, thanks to Italy's economy, which had been torn apart during the six years of war. Ferrari knew he had talent. He had a dream. But he couldn't find a way to put them together. It took a holiday miracle to make it happen.

The first Ferrari—the Tipo 125 S—debuted in 1947 as a race car with a V-12 engine. It didn't take long for Enzo Ferrari's cars to become popular, both on and off the racetrack.

Actually, the "miracle" was an old friend, Luigi Chinetti, who had come home from America with an idea. Chinetti knew Ferrari was disappointed with his career. Ferrari's company had been supporting the racing efforts of other companies, but he yearned to do what he had done best—build cars. As the two men spoke, their voices turning into steam before disappearing into the icy night, Chinetti made his pitch.

"Let's make automobiles," he said. "That is the one thing we are good at."

Ferrari was hooked. His first love had always been racing. That's what led him to work for twenty years at Alfa Romeo, the famous Italian car maker, as a designer, mechanic, and driver. Chinetti had convinced his friend. Ferrari would build the cars, and Chinetti would use the **contacts** he had made in America to sell them.

So a legend was created. Today, the name Ferrari **symbolizes** speed, high performance, and **status**. Ferraris are among the most stylish cars on the road and are **coveted** by collectors, movie stars, professional athletes, and anyone else who appreciates the finest in automotive design and driving excitement. Every Ferrari is built with its founder's love of racing in mind. And even though the company Enzo Ferrari started in that cold, dark office has been sold to Italian automaker Fiat, it continues in Ferrari's racing tradition.

Luigi Chinetti (in helmet) drove a Ferrari to victory in the 1949 Belgian Grand Prix. Here, mechanics and curious fans look at the damage done during the race.

The first Ferrari rolled out of the garage in 1947. Since then, countless models and styles have been offered, each bearing the trademark Cavallino Rampante—or **prancing** stallion—emblem. Some have been simple racing machines, substituting unbelievable speed and power for luxury. Others are **extravagant**, complete with buttery Italian leather interiors and almost every other creature comfort imaginable. Enzo Ferrari may not have favored the tamer versions of his creations, but each one had his racing soul.

As the decades rolled on, Ferrari withstood challenges from other European companies, as well as from American automakers, some of whom borrowed from his designs. The cars produced

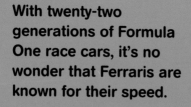

With twenty-two generations of Formula One race cars, it's no wonder that Ferraris are known for their speed.

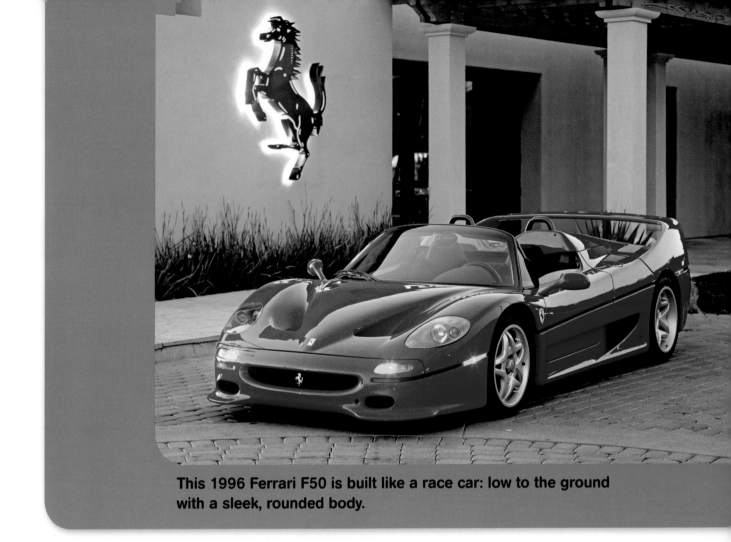

This 1996 Ferrari F50 is built like a race car: low to the ground with a sleek, rounded body.

by Ferrari are celebrations of driving excellence and of Enzo Ferrari's dedication to producing cars that look and move like no other.

The Ferrari story is one of determination and commitment. It tells of one man's vision and how the product of his labor was embraced by those who love cars. The world is filled with cars of every kind. To appreciate the Ferrari, one must understand beauty and style.

CHAPTER TWO

THE MAN BEHIND THE MACHINE

The year was 1908, and Enzo Ferrari was ten years old. His father took him to an automobile race in Bologna, not far from his home in Modena, Italy. He watched two famous Italian drivers, Vincenzo Lancia and Felice Nazzaro, battle for first place in the Circuit of Bologna. He was hooked.

"This race made a great impression on me," he wrote later.

There was no doubt in Enzo's mind what path he wanted to follow. Like Lancia and Nazzaro, he would drive to win. For the next several years he went to many races and became even more interested. Then **tragedy** struck. At age eighteen Ferrari lost his father to **pneumonia** and his brother to another illness. He was alone, and his dream was gone—for a while.

Enzo Ferrari worked with cars for nearly seventy years. He started out as a race car driver and eventually became the founder and president of one of the most famous auto companies in the world!

Alfonso de Portago, a Spanish marquis, drove a Ferrari 375 at the first International Speed Week in Nassau, the Bahamas, in 1954. He won a first and a second place trophy and joined the Scuderia Ferrari racing team the following year.

Even if Ferrari hadn't lost his family, World War I would have interrupted all of their plans. Ferrari became a **blacksmith** in the Italian army. When the war ended, he finally got behind the wheel. And he was good. He joined the Alfa Romeo race team and was considered one of its top drivers until 1923, when he withdrew from the biggest race of his life, the French Grand Prix, Europe's most famous competition. Ferrari never explained his move, but a friend said he lost confidence. Whatever the reason, his full-time racing career was over.

In 1925 Ferrari formed his own company, Scuderia Ferrari, a division of Alfa Romeo that helped racers maintain their cars. Twelve years later

New regulations by the International Federation of Automobiles required that the fuel tank be mounted outside the cockpit, as on this 1957 Ferrari Testarossa.

Even in his eighties, Enzo Ferrari was enthusiastically involved in the business of creating cars.

his firm came under the control of Wilfredo Ricard, a new Alfa Romeo executive who did not get along with Ferrari. Two years later Alfa Romeo fired Ferrari, and he opened Auto Avio Construzione, a company that built race cars. Despite the setback, Ferrari had big plans. This time World War II **intervened**.

By the time the war was over, Italy's economy was near ruin, and few people had the money to buy race cars. Ferrari had reached a **crossroads** once again and was trying to face the reality that he would have to find other work. That was when Chinetti arrived with a plan to keep Ferrari in the race car industry.

As his company grew, Ferrari remained committed to the racing part of the equation. Yes, he adapted to changing times and new tastes, but he was always focused on the driver. He even looked down on those who bought his cars for status.

Ferrari was hard on his customers, and he was also tough to work for. In 1961 several of his employees left to start a rival company. Ferrari didn't bend. He promoted people who stayed with him and fought off challenges from competitors in Europe and America to make sure Ferrari remained one of the most respected brands on the roads and tracks.

In 1970 Ferrari sold the customer car **portion** of his business to Fiat for $11 million and concentrated on racing. Though his team had its share of high and low points, Enzo Ferrari continued to be its soul. In 1988 his flame was finally extinguished. Ferrari died at the age of ninety.

His name will surely live on for decades to come.

The 1950 Ferrari 166 Touring Barchetta was one of the fastest racing cars on the track. It was also a popular street model.

Enzo Ferrari may have needed some help to get his business rolling, but the car maker never lacked self-confidence. He believed there were few people more capable of building better automobiles than he, which was proved by the first models.

A powerful V-12 engine made the 1951 Ferrari a blur on the racetrack.

17

The Tipo 166 Spyder Corsa was one of the earliest cars made by Ferrari. It was based on the Tipo 125 S, but had a larger engine and was easier to handle.

Ferrari didn't decide to build a four-**cylinder** car. An Italian company, Maserati, did that. Six-cylinder autos were out, too. That was the engine Talbot, a British car maker, used. A V-8? Nope, that was Alfa Romeo's engine. Ferrari wanted more power. He wanted more speed. So, his first offering, the Tipo 125 S, had a twelve-cylinder engine. That would be enough. More than enough, really.

But just enough for Ferrari.

Ferrari was committed to creating race cars, but they had to drive smoothly on highways and roads, too. That was the beauty of Ferrari's company. No matter what direction it took, its heart and soul belonged to the track—Ferrari's background.

Despite his love of speed and competition, Ferrari soon realized he had to produce cars people could drive on the roads. So, in 1949, he produced the 166 MM Touring Barchetta, which today remains one of the most important automobiles ever built. The convertible (the Tipo 125 S didn't have a roof) was long in the front, which is why it was called the

As the 1960s dawned, Ferrari went beyond speed and handling to add luxury. The 250 GT SWB Spyder California was an example of that, and the 275 GTB/4 was considered the perfect sports car because it had everything a driver needed. In 1964 the Boxer engine was developed and put in the back of Ferrari models. The engine was so powerful that when it was put into the 365 GT4 Berlinetta ten years later, drivers felt like they were **piloting** an airplane.

The 1961 Ferrari 250 GT SWB Berlinetta was outfitted with a steel body for the road and a smaller alloy body for the race track. SWB stands for "short wheelbase," a feature Ferrari installed to enable the car to go faster.

Ferrari continued to produce more and more power during the rest of the century, with each new model offering more speed, better handling and—in some cases—unparalleled luxury. The car's designs were just as impressive as the engines, with **low-slung** bodies that looked ready to eat up the road. Each was unique and overpowering, and each was worth every penny of its high price tag.

Of course it was. After all, it was a Ferrari.

Early in the morning Ted Mullee discovered "the car." It was the summer of 1955, and he was working the night shift at Ford Motor Company. Mullee **wandered** into a garage on the grounds and saw a magical sight. It was a Ferrari belonging to Henry Ford II, the company chairman and grandson of the founder. But it wasn't just any Ferrari. It was a 1952 212 Touring Barchetta, the last of its kind ever made. The black car gleamed and **radiated** power and style. And Mullee couldn't resist.

The 212 Touring Barchetta features a long front end.

Sports Car International magazine ranked the Ferrari 250 GTO as one of the "Top Sports Cars of the 1960s." The car was also ranked as the greatest Ferrari of all time by *Motor Trend Classic*.

He pushed the car onto the Ford test track, cranked it up, and went for a drive. He didn't know it was Ford's prized possession and a gift from Enzo Ferrari himself. Mullee took about seven or eight high-speed laps, but the roar of the engine alerted his coworkers that the car had been turned loose. For his efforts Mullee received a three-day suspension without pay—and a memory that would last a lifetime.

That 1952 Barchetta represented the end of one of the most famous model lines in automotive history. Introduced in 1949, the Barchetta had a long hood, a short rear deck, an oval grill, and a fiery

A V-12 engine that produced 340 hp made the 1976 Ferrari 400 GT coupe appealing to drivers who wanted an everyday vehicle with a race car personality.

Ferrari's Testarossa line got its name from the red-painted cylinder heads on the engine, as seen in this 1957 model.

red color that would come to be the **distinctive** Ferrari hue. It closed the gap between road cars and race cars, and some historians believe it influenced the design of the Ford Thunderbird. In 1947 the Barchetta was the fastest sports car in the world and evidence that Ferrari had made great progress in just a couple of years.

Only two years earlier, on May 11, 1947, Ferrari had debuted the Tipo 125 S, his first model. The reviews were hardly overwhelming. One newspaper called the Tipo "small, red and ugly." Critics did not know that Ferrari would become the most stylish car of all and would feature future models that would wow the car world.

In 1956 Ferrari introduced the 410 Superamerica, the first Ferrari road car built especially for the U.S. market. Only fourteen were produced—and no wonder. The car cost $16,800, or $10,000 more than a Cadillac Fleetwood Limousine!

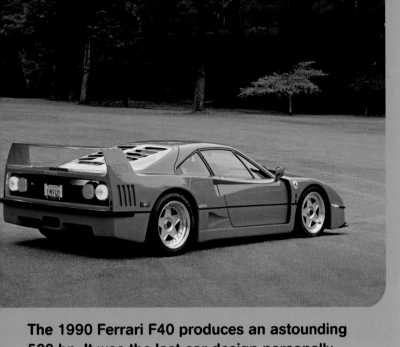

The 1990 Ferrari F40 produces an astounding 500 hp. It was the last car design personally approved by Enzo Ferrari before he died in 1988.

The 250 Gran Turismo Omologato (GTO) was built in 1962 and hit a top speed of 170 miles per hour (273 kilometers per hour). Thirty-nine were produced, and each is now worth between $5.5 and $6 million. The GTO was long in front with a sloped rear and a high windshield and was virtually unbeatable on the road. As powerful as it was, the 250 GT Berlinetta Lusso was **sleek**. Some call it the most beautiful Ferrari ever because of its graceful curves and roomy, luxurious interior.

By the 1970s racing focused on aerodynamics, but Ferrari didn't forget about speed, as the 1974 365 GT4 Berlinetta Boxer proved with a top speed of 210 mph (338 km/h).

With a top speed of over 200 mph (322 km/h) and an undeniably cool look, the 2003 Ferrari Enzo is the perfect tribute to the company's founder.

In 1976 the 400 GT debuted, giving Ferrari a top-of-the-line sedan to compete with Maserati and Mercedes. Then came the Testarossa.

Unveiled in 1984, it became the Ferrari signature car for twelve years. The name *Testarossa*, which means "red head" in Italian, came from the red paint that covered part of the engine. With a lean and low design, it just about screamed, "Speed!" The fortieth anniversary of Ferrari came in 1987 and brought with it the F40. It was nothing fancy; there wasn't even a radio in the car—for good reason. The car was so loud, no one could have heard the radio anyway.

In 1994 Ferrari's F355 combined tremendous handling and speed with top-shelf styling. And if you thought that was fast, the F50 truly turned your head, hitting the road in 1997 and going from 0 to 60 mph (0 to 96 km/h) in a ridiculous 3.7 seconds. The twenty-first century brought more of the same. Ferrari's Superamerica, 612 Scaglietti, F430 Berlinetta, and F430 Spider were all stylish, fast, and beautiful.

Best of all, they were all Ferraris.

The Ferrari F430 Spider debuted in 2004. In true race car style, the car engine is in the rear, not under the front hood.

Vital Statistics

1947 Ferrari 125 Sport

Special Fact: Only two 125 S models were made.

Power: 118 hp
Engine Size: 91.3 ci/1.5L
Engine Type: V-12
Weight: 1,654 lbs (750 kg)
Top Speed: 105 mph (169 km/h)
0–60 mph (0–96.5 km/h): 10 sec

2008 Ferrari F430

Power: 483 hp
Engine Size: 262 ci/4.3L
Engine Type: V-8 DOHC
Weight: 3,190 lbs (1,450 kg)
Top Speed: 196 mph (315 km/h)
0–60 mph (0–96.5 km/h): 3.9 sec

GLOSSARY

blacksmith	A person who makes tools and other items out of iron.
contacts	People who can be helpful.
covet	To want something that is hard to get.
craft	To build something with great skill.
crossroads	A situation in which a person must choose between two paths.
cylinder	The long, rounded chamber in which a piston moves in the engine of a car, providing power. The more cylinders in a motor, the more power it generates.
distinctive	Different from others; set apart.
extravagant	Extremely expensive and over the top.
horsepower	A measure of the power generated by a motor or engine. The greater the horsepower (hp), the higher the speed at which an automobile is able to travel.
intervene	To come between a person and a goal.
invade	To enter forcefully and to conquer.
low-slung	Close to the ground.
pilot	To drive or fly a vehicle.
pneumonia	An infection of the lungs.
portion	A piece of a larger object that is set aside for an individual or group.
prance	To rise up on one's hind legs and move in a lively way.

radiate	To shine brightly.
sleek	Smooth, shiny, and elegant.
status	A high position in society.
symbolize	To be a sign of; to represent.
tragedy	A very sad event.
unveil	To reveal to a person or group for the first time.
wander	To move about without any destination or purpose.

FURTHER INFORMATION

BOOKS

Acerbi, Leonardo. *Ferrari: A Complete Guide to All Models*. St. Paul, MN: Motorbooks, 2006.

Adler, Dennis. *Ferrari: The Road From Maranello*. New York: Random House, 2006.

Nye, Doug. *Ferrari: The Red Dream*. St. Paul, MN: Motorbooks, 2006.

WEB SITES

www.ferrariusa.com

www.ferrarifaqs.com

www.ferrariclubofamerica.org

INDEX

Page numbers in **boldface** are photographs.

About the Author

MICHAEL BRADLEY is a writer and broadcaster who lives near Philadelphia. He has written for *Sports Illustrated for Kids*, *Hoop*, *Inside Stuff*, and *Slam* magazines and is a regular contributor to Comcast SportsNet in Philadelphia.